The World's Best Dirty Jokes

**Ribald.
Timeless.
Graphic.
Shocking.
Outrageous.
Classic.
And
Always
Hilarious!**

Mr. "J"

The
World's
Best
Dirty
Jokes

Drawings by Arthur Robins

BALLANTINE BOOKS · NEW YORK

ISBN 0-345-28658-8

This edition published by arrangement with Lyle Stuart, Inc.

Manufactured in the United States of America

First Ballantine Books Edition: January 1980

*May all your pleasures be long ones—
and may all your days be filled with love.*

Acknowledgments

"Mr. J.," who compiled this book, is grateful to a number of people who helped to judge the jokes that follow:

Morris Cargill (of Jamaica, W.I.)
William M. Gaines
Al Goldstein
Carlos Gonzalez
John Hearne (of Jamaica, W.I.)
Liz Hearne (of Jamaica, W.I.)
Carole Livingston
David Ross
Morris Sorkin
Rory John Stuart
Sandra Lee Stuart
Allan J. Wilson

—and to Dick Manning, Paul Schumer, and the late Frank Edwards, who told us many of them in their masterful manner. . . .

Lakeville, Conn.
July, 1975.

One morning recently
A young woman
Got out of bed
Slipped into her robe
Raised the shade
Uncovered the parrot
Put on the coffee pot
Answered the phone
And heard a masculine voice say:
"Hello, honey. My ship just hit port
And I'm coming right over."
So the young lady
Took the coffee pot off the stove
Covered up the parrot
Pulled down the shade
Took off her robe
Got into bed
and heard the parrot mumble,
"Kee-rist, what a short day that was!"

The World's Best Dirty Jokes

Reggie owned an elephant, but the cost of feeding it was getting out of hand. Then he got an idea. He had seen elephants lift one leg, and even two legs. Once in a circus he'd even seen an elephant lift three legs in the air and stand on just one.

So Reggie announced to the world that he'd pay ten thousand dollars to anyone who could make his elephant stand in the air on no legs. However, each person who wanted to try would have to pay a hundred dollars.

People came from near and far. They tried everything from coaxing to hypnotism, but no one could make the elephant rise up in the air.

Then one day a blue convertible drove up and a little man got out and addressed Reggie: "Is it true that you'll pay ten thousand dollars if I make your elephant get off all four legs?"

"Yes," Reggie said, "but you've got to pay one hundred dollars to try."

The little man handed Reggie a hundred-dollar bill. Then he went back to the car and took out a metal club. He walked up to the elephant and looked him in the eye. Then he walked behind the elephant and swung hard, hitting the elephant smack on the balls. The elephant let out a roar and flew up into the air.

After the little man had collected his ten thousand dollars, Reggie was very depressed. He'd only taken in eight thousand dollars and now he'd not only lost a couple of grand but still had the problem of feeding and housing the elephant.

Suddenly Reggie got another inspiration. He knew that elephants could move their heads up and down, but he had never seen one move from side to side. So he announced that he would pay ten thousand dollars to anyone who could make his elephant move his head from side to side. However, each person who wanted to try would have to pay one hundred dollars.

People came from near and far. They paid their hundred and they tried, but, of course, none succeeded.

Then just when things were going well, a familiar blue convertible drove up and the little man came out. He addressed Reggie: "Is it true that you'll pay me ten thousand dollars if I can make your elephant move his head from side to side?"

"Yes," said Reggie, "but you've got to pay a hundred dollars to try."

The little man handed Reggie the hundred dollars. Then he returned to his car and took out his metal club. He walked up to the elephant.

"Do you remember me?" he asked.

The elephant nodded by shaking his head up and down.

"Do you want me to do it again?"

The elephant quickly shook his head . . . no.

This man was in bed with a married woman when they heard the door open. "Oh my God," she gasped, "it's my husband! Quick, hide in the closet!"

The man hurried into the closet and closed the door. Suddenly, he heard a small voice saying, "It's very dark in here."

"Who is that?" he asked.

"That's my mother out there," the small voice said. "And now I'm going to scream."

"Please don't!" the man said.

"Okay, but it'll cost you money," the boy said.

"Here's five dollars."

"I'm going to scream!" said the small voice.

"Okay, here's ten dollars!"

"I'm going to scream," the small voice said.

"Here's twenty dollars."

Finally, when the boy turned down thirty-five dollars, the man said, "All I have is forty dollars."

"I'll take it!"

At last, the husband left and the man was able to get out of the closet and make a hasty exit.

That afternoon, the mother took the boy with her on a shopping trip.

"I want to get that bicycle," he said.

3

The mother said, "No, you can't. It costs too much money."

The boy said, "I've got forty dollars."

The mother said, "Where would you get forty dollars?"

The boy wouldn't talk. She began to berate him. He refused to respond. She slapped his face. He stood stoicly. Finally, twisting his arm, she dragged him into the nearby neighborhood church and approached the parish priest. "Father, my son has forty dollars and he won't tell me where he got it. Maybe you can find out?"

The priest nodded. He led the boy into a confessional booth. The boy sat on one side and the priest in the other. The boy said, "It's very dark in here. . . ."

And the priest said, "Now, don't you start that again!"

Then there is the story of the eighty-year-old Italian roué who called on his doctor.

"Professore, I would like you to examine me. To see if I am sexually fit."

"Very well, let me see your sex organs, please."

The aged patient replied, "Eccoli," and stuck out his index finger and his tongue.

A man who was frightened of dentists delayed seeing one until he only had six teeth left in his mouth.

The dentist examined him and said: "These teeth are finished. Let me pull them out. Let me do root canal work and all those other things I do, and you'll have a complete new set of choppers in your mouth. Beautiful you'll look, and chewing problems you'll no longer have."

The man was dubious. "I'm a physical coward, Doc. I can't stand the pain."

"Who said anything about pain? I'm a painless dentist!"

"You say it, but how do I know if it's true?"

"Not to worry," the dentist said. "I did a job exactly like this for another man. I'll give you his name and you can phone him right now. Ask if I caused him any pain."

So the man telephoned George Kaplan in Brooklyn.

"Mr. Kaplan," he said, "my name is Al Goldstein. You don't know me, but I'm in the office of your dentist and he says he did a big job on your teeth. Is that correct?"

"Correct it is," Kaplan agreed.

"Okay," said Goldstein. "Now I want you to tell me the honest truth. Did it hurt? Tell me, yes or no?"

"A yes or no I can't give you," said Kaplan, "but I can give you a fr'instance. Every Sunday I go rowing in Prospect Park . . ."

"So?" said Goldstein.

"So," said Kaplan, "our dentist finished with me in December. Now it's June and it's Sunday, and, as usual, I'm in my rowboat on the Prospect Park lake. Suddenly, one of the oars slip away. When I reach over to grab it, my balls get caught in the oarlock. Would you believe it, Mr. Goldstein, it was the first time in six months that my teeth didn't hurt!"

An elephant was having an awful time in the jungle because a horsefly kept biting her near her tail and there was nothing she could do about it. She kept swinging her trunk, but he was far out of reach.

A little sparrow observed this and suddenly flew down and snipped the horsefly in half with his beak.

"Oh, thank you!" said the elephant. "That was such a relief."

"My pleasure, ma'am," said the sparrow.

"Listen, Mr. Sparrow, if there's anything I can ever do for you, don't hesitate to ask."

The sparrow hesitated. "Well, ma'am—" he said.

"What is it," said the elephant. "You needn't be shy with me."

"Well," said the sparrow, "the truth is that all my life I wondered how it would feel to fuck an elephant."

"Go right ahead," said the elephant. "Be my guest!"

The sparrow flew around behind the elephant and began to fuck away. Up above him, a monkey in the tree watched and began to get very excited. He started to masturbate. This shook a coconut loose and it fell from the tree, hitting the elephant smack on the head.

"Ouch!" said the elephant.

At which point, the sparrow looked over from behind and said, "Am I hurting you, dear?"

The late Dr. Kinsey was questioning a group of men about the number of times they had sex relations with members of the opposite sex.

In response to his question, a group of men raised their hands to indicate that they had sex every night. Then some said they had relations ten times a month. A small group said they only did it about four times a month.

Finally, every man in the room had been accounted for except one man who was sitting in the corner.

Dr. Kinsey moved closer to him. "All right. How many of you have sex relations only once a year?"

"Me! Me!" the man piped up, waving his hand wildly and wearing an ear-to-ear smile.

"Fine," said Dr. Kinsey. "But why are you so happy about it?"

"Because tonight's the night!" the man explained with glee. "Tonight's the night!"

So this old man went into Ma Agnew's whorehouse and said, "Listen, Ma, I want a girl with gonorrhea."

The madam nodded and sent him upstairs to a room. Then she called one of her favorites for him. The girl came into the room and started to undress when he asked, "Do you have gonorrhea?"

"Gonorrhea? I should say not!" she said.

The old man sent her back. The madam summoned another girl and said, "Shirley, you go upstairs and tell this old codger that you have the clap. Okay? Let's do what we have to to make him happy."

The girl agreed and went upstairs, and when the old man asked, "Do you have gonorrhea?" she smiled and said, "Of course I do!"

"Good!" he said. "Let's get it on."

They got into bed together and fucked for about ten minutes. When it was over and they lay side by side, the girl named Shirley said, "Listen, grandpa, I've got a confession to make. I don't really have gonorrhea."

The old man smiled. "Now you do," he said.

He went to his doctor full of anger. "Doc," he said, "I feel like killing my wife. You've got to help me. You've got to tell me what to do."

The doctor decided on how to best handle the case. "Look," he said, "here are some pills. You take these twice a day and they'll enable you to fuck your wife six times a day. If you do this for thirty days, you'll fuck her to death."

"Wonderful, doc," said the grateful patient. "I think I'll take her to Miami Beach so there won't be anything to interfere with us and no one will be suspicious."

He left with a bottle of pills in his hand and a smile on his face.

Nearly a month passed. The doctor flew to Miami Beach for a medical convention. There, on Lincoln Road, he saw his patient coming along in a wheelchair, just managing to move forward.

"What happened?" the doctor said. "What happened?"

"Don't worry, doc," the patient reassured him, "two more days and she'll be dead."

An old man made it shakily through the door to Joe Conforte's Mustang Ranch, outside Reno, Nevada.

The receptionist stared at him. "You gotta be in the wrong place," she exclaimed. "What are you looking for?"

"Ain't this the famous Mustang? Ain't this where you allus got forty-five girls ready 'n' able?"

The receptionist looked perplexed. "Ready for what?"

"I want a girl," the old man rasped. "I wanna get laid."

"How old are you, Pop?" she asked.

"Ninety-two," he replied.

"Ninety-two? Pop, you've *had* it!"

"Oh," said the old man, a little disconcerted as his trembling fingers reached for his wallet. "How much do I owe you?"

The scene was Elaine's Restaurant on Second Avenue in Manhattan on a crowded Saturday night. A stranger walked in from the street and pompously announced that, even with a blindfold on, he could identify any wine.

The challenge was immediately accepted. A dark cloth was placed over his eyes and wine after wine was handed to him.

"Lafite-Rothschild, 1958," he would announce. Or, "Bernkasteler Badstube, 1951." And he was always right.

Finally, someone handed him a glass he couldn't identify. He sipped, and then he sipped again. Suddenly he spat it out and pulled off the blindfold.

"Hell, man! This is urine! Plain fresh urine!"

"Yes," said a small voice in the background, "but *whose*?"

This gay chap was looking in a sex shop window. He saw a large rubber cock that appealed to him, and he ventured inside.

When the clerk came to wait on him, he pointed to the big black penis in the window. "I'll take that one," he said.

"Should I wrap it or just put it in a bag?" asked the clerk.

"Neither," said the customer. "I'll just eat it right here."

Jim and Joe were two friends who shared an apartment together in Chicago. One day, Jim came home to find Joe weeping into his hands. "I'm so unlucky! So unlucky!" he moaned.

"You're always saying that, and it isn't so," Jim said.

"It is! It is!" Joe said. "I'm the most unlucky fellow you know!"

"What happened now?"

"Well, I met this beautiful woman on Madison Street. We got to talking and we stopped off at a small bar and had a few drinks. Wow! We got really mellow. When she suggested that I go to her place, I thought my luck had changed."

"It sounds like it did," Jim said.

"Minutes after we entered her apartment I was in bed with her. I was just starting to climax when we heard the door bang open."

"It's my husband!" she said.

"I didn't even have time to grab a towel. I bounded for the window and just managed to climb out, hanging on the ledge by my hands, when he barged in.

"He sized up the scene immediately, and then he saw my hands hanging on for dear life. He came to the window and started pounding my knuckles with a

17

hammer. Then he took out his cock and pissed all over me. Then he slammed the window on my bloody fingers.

Then, as if I didn't have trouble enough, two old ladies on the street saw me hanging there stark naked, and they started screaming for the police. The cops came and I was arrested. Now do you see what I mean when I say I'm unlucky?"

"Nonsense," Jim said. "You're upset, but an experience like that could happen to anyone."

"You don't understand," Joe said, "When the cops come to arrest me, I looked down and my feet were only four inches from the ground. Now do you see what I mean when I say I'm unlucky?"

Jones took his nymphomaniac wife to the doctor for treatment. "This is one hot potato of a lady, doctor," he said. "Maybe you can do something for her? She goes for any man, and I get very jealous."

"We'll see," the doctor said. He directed Mrs. Jones into his examining room, closed the door behind him and told her to undress. Then he told her to get up onto the examining table on her stomach.

The moment he touched her buttocks, she began to moan and squirm. It was too much for him to resist, and he climbed up on top of her and began to screw her.

Jones suddenly heard moans and groans coming from the examination room. Unable to control himself, he pushed open the door, to be confronted by the sight of the doctor astride his wife and banging away.

"Doctor, what are you doing?" he asked.

The flustered doctor said, "Oh, it's you, Jones? I'm only taking your wife's temperature!"

Jones opened his switchblade knife and began to hone it on his sleeve very deliberately. "Doc," he said, "when you take that thing out, it better have numbers on it!"

A midget went into a whorehouse. None of the girls really wanted to serve him, so finally they drew lots and Mitzi was unlucky and went up to the room with him.

A minute later, there was a loud scream. The Madam and all of the girls charged up the staircase and into the room. Mitzi lay on the floor in a dead faint. Standing next to the bed was the midget, nude, and with a three foot cock hanging down and almost touching the floor.

The girls were dumbfounded by the sight. Finally, one of them regained her composure to say, "Sir, would you mind if we felt it? We've never seen anything like that before."

The midget sighed. "Okay, honey. But only touching. No sucking. I used to be six feet tall."

A ventriloquist was driving in the country when he was attracted to a large farm. He asked for and was given a tour.

As he was shown through the barn, the ventriloquist thought he'd have some fun. He proceeded to make one of the horses talk.

The hired hand, wide-eyed with fear, rushed from the barn to the farmer. "Sam," he shouted, "those animals are talking! If that little sheep says anything about me, it's a damned lie!"

The salesman stopped at a farmhouse one evening to ask for room and board for the night. The farmer told him there was no vacant room.

"I could let you sleep with my daughter," the farmer said, "if you promise not to bother her."

The salesman agreed.

After a hearty supper, he was led to the room. He undressed in the dark, slipped into bed, and felt the farmer's daughter at his side.

The next morning he asked for his bill.

"It'll be just two dollars, since you had to share the bed," the farmer said.

"Your daughter was very cold," the salesman said.

"Yes, I know," said the farmer. "We're going to bury her today."

Charlie was visiting an old friend and his wife for dinner. When the time came to leave, his car wouldn't start, and it was too late to call the local service station.

The husband urged Charlie to stay over. There was no spare bed in the house; there wasn't even a sofa. So Charlie would have to sleep with the husband and wife.

No sooner had the husband fallen asleep when the wife tapped Charlie on the shoulder and motioned for him to come over to her.

"I couldn't do that," he whispered. "Your husband is my best friend!"

"Listen, sugar," she whispered back, "there ain't nothing in the whole wide world could wake him up now."

"I can't believe that," Charlie said. "Certainly if I get on top of you and screw you, he'll wake up, won't he?"

"Sugar, he certainly won't. If you don't believe me, pluck a hair out of his asshole and see if that wakes him."

Charlie did just that. He was amazed when the husband remained asleep. So he climbed over to the wife's side of the bed and fucked her. When he

23

finished, he climbed back to his own side. It wasn't long before she tapped him on the shoulder and beckoned him over again. Again he pulled a hair to determine if his old friend was asleep. This went on eight times during the night. Each time Charlie screwed the woman, he first pulled out one of the husband's asshole hairs.

The ninth time he pulled a hair, the husband awoke and muttered: "Listen, Charlie, old pal, I don't mind you fucking my wife, but for Pete's sake, stop using my ass for a scoreboard!"

Muldoon had died from dysentery. When they went to prepare him for burial, he was still excreting. The undertaker thought about it for a moment, then went out and returned with a large cork. He corked up Muldoon's ass.

A couple of hours later, O'Shawnessy and Ryan came to carry the body down to the living room for the wake.

Ryan led the way as they started walking down the stairs slowly. Soft organ music was playing in the background and all the guests stood about with their heads bowed.

Suddenly, the cork came out and excreta came pouring down on top of Ryan's head. He promptly dropped the body and Muldoon's corpse came hurtling down the stairs.

The undertaker rushed up to Ryan. "What the hell did you do, man?"

And Ryan said calmly, "Listen, man, if that bastard can shit, he can walk!"

When the delegate from the emerging African nation was in Moscow, he watched a game of Russian roulette. Someone put the barrel of a pistol to his head and pulled the trigger. One of the six chambers contained a real bullet.

Now the Russian delegate was visiting the African nation.

"We would like to show you our version of roulette," the Ambassador said. "We call this African roulette."

"How do you play it?"

The Ambassador pointed to six buxom African girls sitting in a circle. "Any of these girls will give you a blow job."

"Where is the roulette part? Where is the jeopardy?" the Russian asked.

"Well," said the African Ambassador, "one of the girls is a cannibal."

Little Willie had a gambling problem. He'd bet on anything. One day, Willie's father consulted his teacher.

The teacher said, "Mr. Gaines, I think I know how to teach Willie a real lesson. We'll trap him into a big wager that he'll lose."

Willie's father agreed to cooperate with the plan.

The next day at school, the teacher watched Willie making wagers with the other children, and she said, "Willie, I want you to remain after class."

When the others had left the classroom, Willie walked up to the teacher. Before she could open her mouth, he said, "Don't say it, Miss B.; I know what you're going to say, but you're a liar!"

"Willie!" the startled teacher said. "What are you talking about?"

"You're a fake!" Willie continued. "How can I believe anything you tell me? You've got this blond hair on top, but I've seen your bush and it's pitch black!"

Trying to keep her cool, the teacher said, "Willie, that isn't true."

"I'll bet a dollar it is!" Willie challenged.

The teacher saw her chance to teach Willie his lesson. "Make it five dollars and you have a bet," she said.

"You're on!" Willie whipped out a five-dollar bill.

Before anyone could come into the room, Miss B. dropped her panties, spread her legs, and showed Willie that her pubic hair was as blond as the hair on top of her head.

Willie hung his head. "You win," he said, handing her the fiver.

Miss B. couldn't wait for him to leave so she could get to a phone to call his father. She reported what had happened. "Mr. Gaines," she said, "I think we've finally taught him a lesson."

"The hell we have," the father muttered. "This morning Willie bet me ten dollars that he'd see your cunt before the day was over."

The famous Greek ship owner, Ori Oristotle, was having a house built on a large piece of land in Greece. He said to the architect, "Don't disturb that tree over there because directly under that tree is where I had my first sex."

"How sentimental, Mr. Oristotle," the architect said. "Right under that tree."

"Yes," continued Ori Oristotle, "And don't touch that tree over there either. Because that's where her mother stood watching while I was having my first sex."

"Her mother just stood there while you were fucking her daughter?" the architect asked.

"Yes," said the Greek ship owner.

"But, Mr. Oristotle, what did her mother say?"

"Baaaa."

Mrs. Keller had a very talented parrot. At her dinner parties he was the center of attention, for she had trained him to repeat what the butler said when he announced the guests as they arrived.

The parrot had only one failing: He loved to fuck chickens. Every chance he got, he would fly over the fence into the yard of the farmer next door and fuck his chickens.

The farmer complained to Mrs. Keller, and finally she laid the law down to the parrot.

"Bertram," she said, "you better listen to me! The next time you go into Farmer Whalen's yard and fuck another chicken I'm going to punish you plenty!"

The parrot hung his head to show he understood. But two days later, he couldn't resist temptation and over the fence he went. He was deep into screwing his third hen when Farmer Whalen spotted him and chased him. Whalen compained again to Mrs. Keller.

"Now you're going to get it!" she said. She got a pair of barber's shears and clipped all the feathers from the top of the parrot's head.

That night, Mrs. Keller threw one of her gala parties. She put the parrot on top of the piano.

"Bertram," she said, "you've been a rotten old thing. Tonight you're to sit here all night. No wandering around and no playing the way you usually do!"

And so, feeling rather disconsolate, the parrot sat on the piano. As the butler announced the guests, Bertram performed as usual, repeating the names. The butler said, "Mr. Arnold Levy and Lady Stella," and the parrot said, "Mr. Arnold Levy and Lady Stella." The butler said, "Mr. and Mrs. Robert Salomon," and the parrot said, "Mr. and Mrs. Robert Salomon."

Then two bald-headed men entered the room. Without waiting for the butler to announce them, the parrot shouted: "All right, you chicken-fuckers! Up here on the piano with me!"

A farmer sent his fifteen-year-old son to town and, as a birthday present, handed him a duck. "See if you can get a girl in exchange for this," he said.

The lad met a prostitute and said, "It's my birthday and all I've got is this duck. Would you be willing to—?"

"Sure," she said. "I'm sentimental about birthdays. And besides, I've never owned a duck."

Afterwards, she said, "Do you know, for a fifteen-year-old, you're quite a lay. If you do it again, I'll give you back your duck."

"Sure," said the boy.

When his pleasurable work was through, he started on his way home. While he was crossing the main street in the village, the duck suddenly flew out of his hands and was hit by a passing beer truck. The driver of the truck felt sorry for the boy and gave him $2.

When he got home, his father asked, "How did you make out?"

The son said: "I got a fuck a duck, a duck for a fuck, and two dollars for a fucked-up duck."

Lee and Larry were a pair of winos. They woke up with the shakes one afternoon to find they had only forty cents between them. Lee began to climb the walls, but Larry said calmly, "Look, old man, give me the forty cents and I'll show you how we can drink free all day." So they went into a delicatessen, and Lee bought a frankfurter, which he stuck in Larry's fly.

Next, they went into a nearby bar and ordered drinks. When the bartender asked for his money, Lee got down on the floor and started sucking the frankfurter. The bartender screamed, "You fucking queers, get out of here!"

They repeated the scene in bar after bar until they had toured a dozen of them. Finally, Lee complained, "Listen, Larry, it was a great scheme but my knees are getting sore from hitting the floor so much."

Larry shook his head. "You should complain," he said. "We lost the hot dog after the second bar!"

Inflation was getting out of hand so Joe suggested to his wife, Louise, that they try a unique way to save some money on the side.

"Every time I lay you, I'll give you a dollar for your piggy bank," he said.

A few weeks later, they decided to open the piggy bank. Out tumbled a bunch of dollars, but these were mixed with a rich cluster of fives, tens and twenties.

"Louise," asked Joe, "where did you get all that money? Each time we fucked I only gave you a dollar."

"So?" she said. "Do you think everyone is as stingy as you?"

The agent for a beautiful actress discovered one day that she had been selling her body at a hundred dollars a night.

The agent, who had long lusted for her, hadn't dreamed that she had been so easily obtainable. He approached her, told her how much she turned him on and how much he wanted to make it with her.

She agreed to spend the night with him, but said he would have to pay her the same hundred dollars that the other customers did.

He scratched his head, considered it, and then asked, "Don't I even get my agent's ten percent as a deduction?"

"No siree," she said. "If you want it, you're going to have to pay full price for it, just like the other johns."

The agent didn't like that at all, but he agreed.

That night, she came to his apartment after her performance at a local night club. The agent screwed her at midnight, after turning out all the lights.

At 1 A.M. she was awakened again. Again she was vigorously screwed. In a little while, she was awakened again, and again she was screwed. The actress was impressed with her lover's vitality.

"My God," she whispered in the dark, "you are

virile. I never realized how lucky I was to have you for my agent."

"I'm not your agent, lady," a strange voice answered. "He's at the door taking tickets!"

A drunk walked into a bar crying. One of the other men at the bar asked him what happened.

"I did a horrible thing," sniffled the drunk. "Just a few hours ago I sold my wife to someone for a bottle of scotch."

"That *is* awful," said the other guy. "And now she's gone and you want her back, right?"

"Right," said the drunk, still crying.

"You're sorry you sold her because you realized too late that you love her, right?"

"Oh, no," said the drunk. "I want her back because I'm thirsty again!"

The butcher lived in an apartment over his shop. One night he was awakened by strange noises coming from below. He tiptoed downstairs and observed that his 19-year-old daughter was sitting on the chopping block and masturbating with a liverwurst. He sighed and tiptoed back to bed.

The next morning, one of his customers came in and asked for some liverwurst. The butcher explained that he didn't have any.

The lady was annoyed. She pointed and said, "No liverwurst, eh? Well, what's that hanging on the hook right over there?"

The butcher frowned at her and replied, "That, lady, is my son-in-law."

The couple visited a sex clinic to complain that their sex life had become a bore.

Each night the man would arrive home. His wife would prepare supper. After supper, they'd watch two hours of TV. Immediately after the eleven o'clock news, they would get into bed. From that point on, every move was routine.

"No wonder," the sex consultant said. "You've made sex monotonous. Stop living on a schedule. Get into sex when you feel like it. Don't wait until eleven o'clock each night. Do it when you get into the mood."

The couple agreed to try the advice. They returned the following week.

"How did things work out?" the sex doctor asked.

The man and his wife were beaming. "It worked! It worked!"

"Tell me about it," said the doctor.

"Well, two nights after we saw you, we were eating supper when I noticed that although it was only eight-thirty, I had this great erection. Sweetie pie here was staring at it with longing eyes. So I didn't wait for any shower or any news broadcast. Instead, I reached out, ripped off her blouse and her bra. Then I pulled off her panties. I flung her to the floor right under the table. Then I unzipped my fly and pulled out my cock and we began to fuck. Man, we fucked like we have never fucked before."

"That's wonderful!" said the sex expert. "I told you it would work if you did it when the spirit moved!"

"Only one thing," the man said a little sadly. "They're not going to let us come back to Howard Johnson's restaurant any more."

A mother and her daughter came to the doctor's office. The mother asked the doctor to examine her daughter.

"She has been having some strange symptoms and I'm worried about her," the mother said.

The doctor examined the daughter carefully. Then he announced, "Madam, I believe your daughter is pregnant."

The mother gasped. "That's nonsense!" she said. "Why, my little girl has nothing whatsoever to do with men." She turned to the girl. "You don't, do you, dear?"

"No, Mumsy," said the girl. "Why, you know that I have never so much as kissed a man!"

The doctor looked from mother to daughter, and back again. Then, silently he stood up and walked to the window. He stared out. He continued staring until the mother felt compelled to ask, "Doctor, is there something wrong out there?"

"No, Madam," said the doctor. "It's just that the last time anything like this happened, a star appeared in the East and I was looking to see if another one was going to show up."

The state senator was seeking votes for his election campaign for Congress and decided to visit the local Indian reservation. He stood in the large community hall and told the Indians what he would do for them if he was elected.

"I think the time has come when you people deserve to really control your own destiny," he said.

From the crowded auditorium came a responding chorus, "Um gwalla gwalla!"

The senator smiled. "Furthermore," he continued, "I think the time has come for your old people to get really good pensions."

Again came a chorus of "Um gwalla gwalla!"

He nodded approvingly. "One more thing," he said, "if I'm elected, I'm not going to rest until every one of you Indians get full citizenship with all the rights every full-blooded American has."

Once again, there was a loud responding roar of "Um gwalla gwalla!"

After his speech, the senator was given a guided tour of the reservation. He saw a high fence and asked what it contained.

The guide said: "That the place where we kept bulls. Now just empty grazing ground. No bulls now."

"Good!" he said, and started to climb over the fence.

His guide warned: "Be careful, senator! You go in there you liable to step in much um gwalla gwalla."

The parish priest couldn't resist the pretty young girl. She was reciting her confession, and it was all too much for him. He told her to come with him to his room. There, he placed his arm around her.

"Did the young man do this to you?" he asked.

"Yes, Father, and worse," the girl replied.

"Hmm," said the priest. He kissed her.

"Did he do this?"

"Yes, Father, and worse," the girl said.

"Did he do this?" the priest asked, and he lifted her skirt and fingered her bush.

"Yes, Father, and worse."

By this time, the priest was thoroughly aroused. He pulled the girl down onto the rug and inserted his penis, breathing heavily as he asked, "Did he manage to do this?"

"Yes, Father, and worse," said the girl.

When the priest had finished with the girl, he asked, "He did this too, and worse? My dear daughter, what worse could he have done?"

"Well," the shy young girl said, "I think, Father, that he's given me gonorrhea."

Little Red Riding Hood was walking through the woods on her way to visit her grandmother, when suddenly a wolf jumped out from behind a tree.

"Ah-ha!" the wolf said, "Now I've got you. And I'm going to eat you!"

"Eat! Eat! Eat!" Little Red Riding Hood said angrily. "Damn it! Doesn't anybody fuck anymore?"

The Frenchman and the Italian were in the woods hunting together when suddenly a voluptuous blonde girl raced across their path, totally nude.

"Would I love to eat that? *Oui, oui!*" the Frenchman said, smacking his lips.

So the Italian shot her.

He had heard that a certain whorehouse in Great Neck, New York, had an unusual reputation for the bizarre. So he drove to the place and, once inside, asked the Madam if she had anything unusual for him to try.

"Things are pretty slow today," she said, "but I do have one number you might enjoy." She went on to describe a New Jersey hen that had been trained to do blow jobs.

"We've got her here, but only for the day."

The visitor could hardly believe it, but he paid the fee and went into a room with the hen. After a frustrating hour of trying to force his cock into the hen's mouth, he figured out that he was dealing with nothing but a plain old chicken. He left.

Thinking about it later, he decided that he had had so much fun trying that he returned the next day and asked the Madam, "Do you have anything new today?"

"Come this way," she said, and led him to a dark room where a group of men were looking through a one-way mirror. He saw that they were watching a girl trying to make it with a dog.

"Wow!" he said to the man standing next to him. "This is really great!"

The man replied, "Man, it ain't nothin'! You shoulda been here yesterday and seen the guy with the chicken."

The recruit had just arrived at a Foreign Legion post in the desert. He asked his corporal what the men did for recreation.

The corporal smiled wisely and said, "You'll see."

The young man was puzzled. "Well, you've got more than a hundred men on this base and I don't see a single woman."

"You'll see," the corporal repeated.

That afternoon, thre hundred camels were herded in the corral. At a signal, the men seemed to go wild. They leaped into the corral and began to screw the camels.

The recruit saw the corporal hurrying past him and grabbed his arm. "I see what you mean, but I don't understand," he said. "There must be three hundred of those camels and only a hundred of us. Why is everybody rushing? Can't a man take his time?"

"What?" exclaimed the corporal, startled. "And get stuck with an ugly one?"

She was wearing a very tight skirt, and when she tried to board the Fifth Avenue bus she found she couldn't lift her leg. She reached back and unzipped her zipper. It didn't seem to do any good, so she reached back and unzipped it again.

Suddenly the man behind her lifted her up and put her on the top step.

"How dare you?" she demanded.

"Well, lady," he said, "by the time you unzipped my fly for the second time I thought we were good friends."

This Chinese laundryman complained to the doctor that he was very constipated. The doctor gave him a prescription for a good physic. "Come to my office in a few days," said the doctor, "and let me know how it works."

A few days later, the Chinaman visited the doctor.

"Have you moved yet?" asked the doctor.

"No, sir, me no moovee, me no moevee."

The doctor scratched his head and then gave the man a prescription for twice as much. Three days later, when the man reported to the doctor again, he said that he still hadn't moved and the doctor gave him a triple dose, and he said, "Come back to see me in two days and let me know just what is happening."

Two days later, the man came back.

"Well," said the doctor, "have you moved yet?"

"No, sir, me no moovee yet. Me moovee tomorrow, though. House full of shit."

This fellow rushed into a crowded tavern on Saturday night. Men and women stood three-deep at the bar. Our man, who felt nature calling strongly, looked about him but couldn't see anything that resembled a john.

He saw a stairway and bounded up the steps to the second floor in his increasingly desperate search. Just as his bowels threatened to erupt, he spotted a one-foot by one-foot hole in the floor. Now, at the end of his control, he decided to take advantage of the hole. He dropped his pants, hunched over it, and did his thing.

Thoroughly relieved and relaxed, he sauntered down the steps to find, to his surprise, that the bar which had been so crowded a few minutes ago, was now empty.

"Hey!" he yelled to the seemingly empty room, "Where is everyone?"

From behind the bar a voice responded, "Where were you when the shit hit the fan?"

A man went to have plastic surgery on his penis. The surgeon examined him and asked, "What happened?"

"Well, doc, I live in a trailer camp," the man explained, "And from where I am I can see this lovely chick next door. She's blonde and she's built like a brick shithouse. She's so horny that every night I see her take a hot dog from the refrigerator and stick it in a hole in the floor of her trailer. Then she gets down and masturbates herself on the hot dog."

"And?" prompted the doctor.

"Well," said the man, "I felt this was a lot of wasted pussy, so one day I got under the trailer and when she put the hot dog in the hole, I removed it and substituted my dick.

"It was a great idea and everything was going real good, too. Then someone knocked at her door, and she jumped off my hot dog and tried to kick it under the stove."

A population control program had been introduced to the island, but the medical men were having trouble getting the women to take their birth control pills. They decided, therefore, to concentrate on teaching the men to wear condoms.

One of the men who came in had had eight children in eight years, and the doctor told him that he absolutely had to wear a sheath. He explained that as long as he wore it his woman could not have another baby.

About a month later, the wife came in and she was pregnant. The doctor got very angry. He called the man in and gave him a long lecture through an interpreter.

He asked the man why he hadn't worn the sheath. The interpreter said, "He swears he did wear it. He never took it off." The doctor shook his head. "In that case, ask him how in the hell his wife is pregnant again?"

"He says," said the interpreter, "that after six days he had to take a piss so badly that he cut the end off."

Jordan was young and he was horny. When he arrived at the Foreign Legion post he was disturbed by the total absence of females on the post.

"Jeepers, creepers!" he said to the sergeant. "Don't you fellows have any sex here?"

"Sure we do," said the sergeant. "It's just that we of the French Foreign Legion have to adapt to our environment."

"I don't understand."

"Well," the sergeant explained, "the camels come every Thursday afternoon at three o'clock."

"Camels!" the young man snorted in disgust "Huh!"

But by Thursday, he couldn't wait. He stood at the edge of the camp scanning the horizon.

At ten to three, he could see a cloud of dust. It grew larger, and then a herd of about twenty camels came thundering into the camp.

Jordan couldn't wait. Grabbing the first one by the bridle, he quickly began to fuck it.

The sergeant ran up to him. "Private Jordan, what in hell are you doing?"

"Christ, sergeant, it's easy enough to see!"

"No, no, you fool! The camels come to take us to town so we can get the girls!"

Jim Buckley went to a farm to visit his country cousin. He went into the barn to watch the country cousin attach the udders of a cow to the milking machine. The machine went up and down and milk poured out.

Buckley was fascinated. As soon as his country cousin left the barn on some errand, he decided to attach the machine to his penis to see how it would feel.

Two hours later, the country cousin returned to find Buckley lying on the floor and moaning, "Ohhhhhh. Let me out! Let me out!"

"Land's sake," the country cousin exclaimed. "What's goin' on?"

"Can't you see?" Buckley said. "I stuck my prick in your damned machine and turned it on. This is the eighty-seventh time I've come! And I can't seem to turn it off!"

The country cousin scratched his head. "Jim, I'm afraid I can't turn it off either. But don't you worry. We'll feed you and fan you, and the thing's only set for four quarts."

So this elderly couple were sitting in their tiny cold water flat on the lower East Side when the husband said, "Doris, we're in bad shape. Inflation has eaten up our Social Security check. The next one isn't due for a week and we've got no money left for food."

"Could I do anything to help?" she asked.

"Yes," he said. "I hate to see you do this but it's the only way. You're going to have to go out and hustle."

"Me?" she said. "At the age of sixty-five?"

"It's the only way," he said.

Resigned to the situation, she went out into the warm night.

She came staggering in early the next morning.

"How did you do?" asked the husband.

"Here," she said, "I've got four dollars and ten cents."

"Four dollars and ten cents," he said. "Who gave you the ten cents?"

"Everybody," she said.

Garfield Goldwater made a great deal of money in the men's clothing business in New York. He gave to all the charities, attended all the fancy balls, had his name in Earl Wilson's column twice a week—and still wasn't happy. In fact, he was becoming so depressed that a friend suggested he see a psychiatrist.

The psychiatrist listened and then said: "Look here, Mr. Goldwater. You've made all this money, but your success is meaningless because you don't do anything for pleasure. Isn't there anything at all you've always wanted to do? A childhood fantasy? A juvenile ambition?"

"Well," said Garfield Goldwater a little reluctantly, "when I was a boy I wanted to go into the jungle on a safari. You know, kind of like Tarzan did."

The psychiatrist advised: "If that's what you wanted to do, then do it. Life is short and the grave is deep. Do it, man, and do it now!"

Garfield decided to take the advice. Two days later, he flew to Africa, where he confronted the world's most famous gorilla safari hunter.

Patient, the safari hunter explained that he'd retired. However, Garfield Goldwater was not easily put off. "Please, Mr. Safari Hunter," he said, "make one

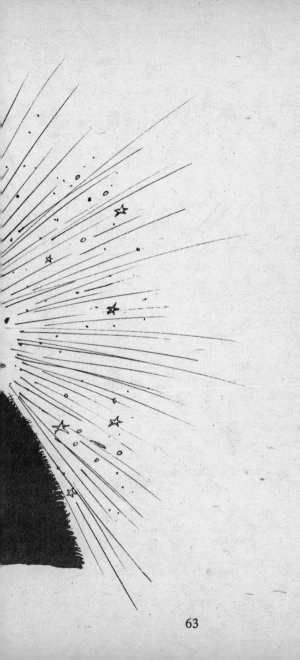

more safari. I'll pay anything you ask. I'm a rich man. Money is no object."

The safari hunter was moved. "I've heard of you," he said. "I've even worn your suits." He thought awhile. Then he asked: "Do you mean what you said about money being no object?"

"Absolutely," vowed Garfield Goldwater.

"All right, here's the deal. In addition to me, you'll need a Zulu, a dog, and a pigmy with a gun. It will cost you ten thousand dollars."

Garfield Goldwater whistled. "Ten thousand dollars!" he exclaimed. "That's a lot of cabbage."

"Only if you don't have it," the safari hunter reminded him.

So Garfield agreed.

The troupe was rounded up, and on the very next afternoon the safari went out on its first mission. Within an hour, the hunter spotted a gorilla in a tree. Everyone stood by while the Zulu climbed the tree. He shook the branches until the gorilla lost his grip and fell to the ground. The dog immediately jumped on the gorilla and bit his penis, at which point the gorilla fainted. A net was slung over him and Garfield had his first gorilla.

He was very pleased. But that night in his tent, Garfield Goldwater thought again about the fee. He went to the safari hunter's tent and awakened him. "I hate to bother you at this hour," he said, "because first, you've done a great job, and second, I'm happy about the gorilla, but third, I think you're taking advantage of me. Ten thousand . . ."

The safari hunter shrugged. "Mr. Goldwater, a deal is a deal."

"I can understand," said Garfield, "the need for the Zulu and the dog. But why do we need the pigmy with the gun? You're padding the bill a little, old man."

There was no response. The safari hunter had fallen asleep.

The next afternoon, they went out and spotted a

larger gorilla in a tree. The Zulu climbed the tree and shook the branches until the gorilla lost his grip and fell to the ground. The dog jumped on the gorilla and bit him on the penis; the gorilla fainted and the safari hunter threw a net over him.

Again Garfield was impressed. But again he began to stew about the high fee. He went to the safari hunter's tent and said: "I want a showdown. I want you to get rid of the pigmy with the gun and reduce my bill."

"Mr. Goldwater," said the safari hunter, "you made a deal. A deal is a deal and that's the deal."

Distraught, Garfield Goldwater returned to his tent. He tried to dream of suits made by Angelo in Rome and ice cream sundaes at Bishoff's in Teaneck, New Jersey, but always his thoughts returned to the ten-thousand-dollar fee and the pigmy with the gun.

The next day, the safari went out, and now it was Garfield Goldwater himself who spotted the gorilla. This time it was a very large one. The Zulu climbed the tree and shook the branches. The Zulu and the gorilla confronted each other, and the two began to wrestle. Suddenly, the gorilla threw the man.

As the Zulu came tumbling down to the ground, he screamed to the pigmy: "Shoot the dog! Shoot the dog!"

Muza Dai Boo, an Arab merchant, was in the marketplace one day when he felt terrible cramps. He just couldn't control him, and let out a long, loud fart.

People stared at him from all sides. Mortally embarrassed, he ran back to his home, packed a few belongings and journeyed far away. For years he traveled from town to town, but always avoided his home town.

At last, an old and weary man, he decided to return. He had grown a long beard and his face had aged enough so that he was sure he would not be recognized. His heart longed for the old familiar streets.

Once in town, he went directly to the marketplace. There, to his surprise, he saw that the street had been paved. He turned to the man nearest him and said, "My friend, how smooth this street is. When, by the grave of Allah, was it so neatly paved?"

"Oh, that," said the man. "That was done three years, four months and two days after Muza Dai Boo farted in the marketplace."

The eighty-eight-year-old millionaire married a four-teen-year-old country girl. He was quite content, but after a few weeks she told him that she was going to leave him if she didn't get some fucking real soon.

He had his chauffeured limousine take him to a high-priced specialist who studied him and then gave him a shot of spermatozoa. "Now look," the doctor said, "The only way you're going to get it hard is to say 'beep,' and then to get it soft again, you say 'beep beep.'"

"How marvelous," the old man said.

"Yes, but I must warn you," the doctor said, "it's only going to work three times before you die."

On his way home, the old man decided he wasn't going to live through three of them anyway, so he decided to waste one trying it out.

"Beep!" he said.

Immediately, his penis got hard.

Satisfied, he said "beep, beep," and his penis got soft again. He chuckled with delight and anticipation.

At that moment, a little yellow Volkswagen pulled past his limousine and went "beep," and the car in the opposite lane responded with "beep beep."

Alert to his jeopardy, the old man instructed his chauffeur to "speed it up." He raced into the house as fast as he could for his last great fuck. "Honey," he shouted at her, "don't ask any questions. Just drop your clothes and hop into bed."

Caught up in his excitement, she did. He undressed nervously and hurried in after her. Just as he was climbing into the bed, he said "beep," and his penis leaped to erection.

He was just starting to put it in when his tender young wife said, "What's all this 'beep beep' shit?"

The teacher walked into the classroom to find words like "cunt" and "cock" scrawled all over the blackboard.

"Children," she said, addressing the classroom. "You are much too young to use vile language like that. Now we're all going to close our eyes and count up to fifty. Then, while our eyes are closed, I want the little boy or girl who wrote those words on the board to tiptoe up and erase them."

At the signal, the teacher and the children all closed their eyes. Then the teacher counted out loud, very slowly.

When she reached fifty, she said, "All right. Everybody open their eyes."

All eyes went to the blackboard.

None of the words were erased. But below them was the message: "Fuck you, teacher. The Phantom strikes again!"

Silas and Sally were out in the cornfield happily fucking away. It had rained that morning and there was lots of mud on the ground, and they found themselves sliding around a bit in the mud.

"Say, honey, is my cock in you or in the mud?" Silas asked.

Sally felt around and said, "Why, Silas, it's in the mud!"

"Well, put it back in you," he said.

After awhile, Silas asked again, "Honey, is it in you or in the mud?"

"In me, honey. In me," Sally cooed happily.

"Well, would you mind putting it back in the mud?"

The teacher told the students that they were going to play a game.

"I've got something behind my back and I'm going to describe it and you guess what it is," she said.

"I'm holding something round and red. Can someone guess?"

"An apple?" little Herbie said.

"No," said the teacher, "but it shows you were thinking. It's a cherry. Now I'm holding something round and orange. Can you tell me what it is?"

"An orange?" little Herbie said.

"No," said the teacher, "but it shows you were thinking. It's a peach."

Herbie raised his hand. "Teacher, can I play the game too?"

The teacher said yes, and Herbie went to the back of the room, faced the rear and said, "Teacher, I'm holding something about two inches long with a red tip."

The teacher said, "Herbie!"

"No," said little Herbie, "but it shows you were thinking. It's a match."

It happened in Paris in the spring. On a sunny day in May, a Chinaman picked up a whore on the Champs Elysées and took her to the Meurice Hotel.

They opened the windows and the breeze blew in and everything seemed beautiful. The Chinaman got into bed with the whore. He fucked her for awhile and then said, *"Pardonnez-moi, Mademoiselle, je suis fatigué."*

So saying, he went to the window and took a deep breath. Then he went under the bed, came out the other side, and jumped into bed to screw again.

After awhile, he got up saying, *"Pardonnez-moi, Mademoiselle, je suis fatigué."* Again he went to the window, took a deep breath, rolled under the bed and came out the other side.

The sixth time this happened, the whore had become very tired too. Getting out of bed, she said *"Pardonnez-moi, Monsieur, je suis fatiguée."*

She went to the open window, took a deep breath, and looked under the bed. She found four other Chinamen there.

One Friday afternoon, Harold's boss told him that he'd have to work overtime that day. That was okay with Harold except that he had no way of letting his wife know he'd be late coming home, since they had just moved into a new little house in the suburbs and didn't have a phone yet.

"Since I'm passing that way, I'll tell her," the boss volunteered.

A few hours later, the boss arrived at the cottage and rang the doorbell. Harold's wife came to the door wearing a see-through wraparound. The boss couldn't take his eyes off her body.

"Yes?" she said.

"I'm Harold's boss," Harold's boss said. "He's working overtime and asked me to tell you he'll be home late."

"Thank you," she said.

"How about going upstairs for some fucking?"

Harold's wife felt her cheeks flush to an angry red. "How dare you!"

The boss shrugged. "Supposing I give you fifty dollars?"

"Absolutely not! Why, I never heard such nerve . . ."

"One hundred dollars?"

"Uh . . . no."

"One hundred and fifty?"

"I don't think that would be right, do you?"

At this point, the boss purred, "Listen, honey, Harold isn't gonna know. It's an easy way to make a hundred and fifty bucks and we'll just spend a little time together."

She nodded, took him by the hand, and led him upstairs to the bed where they had fun and games for an hour.

That night, when Harold came home, he asked, "Did the boss come by and tell you I'd be late?"

"Yes, Harold," the sweet thing said, "he did stop by for a few seconds."

"Good," said Harold. "Then he gave you my salary?"

Benson had been with prostitutes everywhere in the world, but in Hong Kong he met his undoing. He fucked a very sick Chinese whore and picked up so many venereal diseases that the doctors had difficulty separating and identifying them all.

He went to a prominent gynecologist in the American quarter who examined him and shook his head. "Bad news, Benson. You must have immediate surgery and we've got to cut your penis off."

Benson went into traumatic shock at the prognosis. Gathering himself together, he went across the street to another American doctor. There he was told the same thing.

He went out into the street in a daze. Stumbling along, he found himself in the Chinese quarter, where he saw a sign identifying the office of a Chinese surgeon.

Deciding to have one more medical opinion, Benson went in. He told the Chinese doctor that he'd been to two American doctors and both of them wanted to perform immediate surgery to cut off his cock.

The Chinese surgeon examined Benson's penis. He consulted large medical books. Then he examined it again.

"Is there any hope, doc?" Benson asked, plaintively.

"Sure is hope!" the doctor said. "I make complete examination. I know just what's wrong. You play with Chinese girl, but she very sick. You make mistake and go to American doctor. Trouble with American doctors, they always think money, money, money."

Benson brightened up. "You mean I don't need surgery? My penis doesn't have to be cut off?"

"Forget what they say. Go home," the Chinese doctor repeated. "No surgery. Go home. Wait two, maybe three weeks. Pecker fall off all by himself."

A man took his wife to a Broadway show. During the first act intermission, he had to urinate in the worst way. He hurried to the back of the theatre and searched in vain for the men's room.

At last he came upon a fountain surrounded by pretty foliage. He realized that he had wandered back-stage. Noting that no one was around, and in desperation, he opened his pants and pissed into the fountain.

He had difficulty finding his way back to the auditorium, and by the time he sat down next to his wife, the curtain was up and actors were moving about on the stage.

"Did I miss much of the second act?" he whispered.

"Miss it?" she said, "You were in it!"

The man was dining in a very swank restaurant in New York City. When the elderly waiter brought the consommé the customer saw that his thumb was deep in the soup bowl.

Next, the waiter served *steak Diane,* and now his thumb was deep in the gravy. The customer held his tongue. This was, after all, one of New York's finest restaurants.

Finally, for dessert, the waiter brought out *coupe marron.* This time his finger was not in the ice cream.

The customer could contain himself no longer. "Sir," he said to the waiter, "would you tell me why you put your finger in the consommé and the steak gravy, but not in the *coupe marron?*"

The waiter stared coldly at him for a moment, and then replied, "Simple, my good man. I have a bad case of arthritis and warm things relieve the pain in my thumb."

The customer became very angry. "You son-of-a-bitch!" he said, "Putting your thumb in my food! You should take that thumb and ram it up your ass!"

The waiter looked at him dourly and said, "That's what I do in the kitchen."

Do you know the difference between a cocksucker and a corned beef sandwich?

No.

Good. Come over tomorrow for lunch.

The Japanese-American was a long-time customer at this Greek restaurant because he had discovered that they made especially tasty fried rice. Each evening he'd come in he would order "flied lice."

This always caused the Greek restaurant owner to nearly roll on the floor with laughter. Sometimes he'd have two or three friends stand nearby just to hear the Japanese customer order his "flied lice."

Eventually, the customer's pride was so hurt that he took a special diction lesson just to be able to say "fried rice" correctly.

The next time he went to the restaurant, he said very plainly, "Fried rice, please."

Unable to believe his ears, the Greek restaurant owner said, "Sir, would you repeat that?"

The Japanese-American replied: "You heard what I said, you fluckin Gleek!"

The Israeli army unit was crossing the desert and most of the men were on camels. Lt. Smith had a very stubborn camel, and finally it stopped dead in its tracks and refused to move another step.

The rest of the unit moved on, leaving Smith along with his mulish camel.

Smith sat on the camel for three hours. He kicked the camel. He pleaded with the camel. He shouted curses at the camel. But the camel wouldn't move.

He dismounted, and was standing disconsolately at its side when a woman soldier drove up in a jeep. She asked Lt. Smith what the trouble was, and he explained the camel wouldn't budge.

"Oh, I can fix that," she said, jumping out of her jeep. She reached down and put her hand under the camel's belly. The camel jumped up and down, up again, and then suddenly raced away at the rate of half a mile a minute.

Lt. Smith was astounded. "What did you do, lady? What's the trick?"

"It's simple, Lieutenant. I just tickled his balls."

"Well, lady, you'd better tickle mine too, and quickly, because I've got to catch that camel!"

A man was asked by his wife to buy a live chicken for a special dinner. He bought the chicken and was on his way home when he remembered that he didn't have his house key and his wife wouldn't be there for a few hours.

He decided to pass the time by going to a movie. In order to get into the cinema, he stuffed the chicken into his trousers.

He sat down and began watching the movie. It fascinated him so that he didn't notice the chicken sticking its head through his fly.

Two women were sitting next to him, and one of them nudged the other. "Look," she said, "look at that thing there sticking out of the man's pants."

The other replied, "If you've seen one, you've seen them all."

The first one said, "Yes, but this one is eating my popcorn!"

Three nuns were walking along the street and one was describing with her hands the tremendous grapefruit she'd seen in Florida.

The second one, also with her hands, described the huge bananas she'd seen in Jamaica.

The third nun, a little deaf, asked, "Father who?"

So there were these two blacks from a Southern town and they wanted women desperately but couldn't find any. They were driving along the country road when they spotted a pig. One of them jumped out, scooped up the pig and stuck it on the seat between them.

They continued to chug along in their 1963 Ford when a police siren suddenly sounded behind them. A glance at the rear view mirror showed them that a police car was in hot pursuit. They pulled over to the side. Not wanting to be caught with a stolen pig, they tossed a blanket over it.

The officer came up to the side of their car. "What are you up to?" he asked.

"We were just out looking for women," one of the lads replied truthfully.

Suddenly the pig stuck its face through the folds of the blanket.

The cop stared, shook his head sadly, and said, "Lady, can you tell me what a nice Southern girl like you is doing with these two blacks?"

A man was standing on a train platform seeing the train off and he observed someone near him shouting at one of the departing passengers, "Goodbye. Your wife was a great lay! Your wife was a great lay!"

He was stunned.

After the train pulled away, he walked over to the man who'd done the shouting, and asked, "Did I hear you correctly? Did you tell that man his wife was a great lay?"

The other man shrugged his shoulders. "It isn't really true," he said, "but I don't want to hurt his feelings."

The little boy was sitting on the curb crying and an old man who was passing by came over to him.

"What's the matter, little boy?" he asked. "Why are you crying?"

The little boy said, "I'm crying because I can't do what the big boys do."

The old man sat down on the curb and cried too.

Some Americans were touring the marketplace and one of them saw a man on the ground brushing his camel.

"Excuse me, sir," the American said. "Do you know the time?"

The Arab looked at the American. Then he reached over and held the camel's balls, moving them slightly.

"Ten after two," he said, at last.

"My word!" said the American. He caught up to his tour group and insisted some of the others return with him. "You've never seen anything like this!" he promised.

The group went back with him. Again he asked for the time. Again the Arab camel driver reached for the camel's balls. He seemed to be weighing them as he moved them to and fro. Finally, he announced: "Twenty-one minutes past two."

The others were amazed. They went on their way, but the original discoverer of the miracle time-teller remained. He leaned over. "Listen," he confided to the Arab. "I'd give anything to know how you do that. I'll give you twenty American dollars if you show me how you tell the time."

The Arab camel driver thought for a moment, and then nodded. Pocketing the twenty-dollar bill, he beckoned for the American to kneel down where he was. Then he took the camel's balls and gently moved them to the side, out of the way.

"Do you see that clock over there?" he asked.

He was a junior bank executive and he had swindled one hundred thousand dollars from his bank—all of which he'd lost at the races. The bank examiners were coming the next day, and when he confessed the whole thing to his wife, she packed her bags and left him. Totally despondent, he walked to a nearby bridge and stood at the edge of it about to jump off and end it all.

Suddenly a voice called, "Young man, don't do that! There is no need to end your life! I'm a witch and I can help you!"

"I doubt it," he said sadly, "I've stolen a hundred thousand dollars from the bank, for which I'll probably be arrested tomorrow, and my wife has left me."

"Young man, witches can do anything," she said. "I'm going to perform a witch miracle." She said, *"Alakazam!* The hundred thousand dollars has been replaced and there's another hundred thousand in your safe deposit box! *Alakazam!* Your wife is back home again!"

He looked at her in disbelief, "Is this all true?" he asked.

"Of course," she said, "but to keep it true you must do one thing."

"Anything!" he said, "Anything!"

"You must take me to a motel and have sexual intercourse with me."

He stared at her. Se was an ugly old crone, dressed in rags. Nevertheless, he agreed to her terms. He took her to a motel and screwed her all night. In the morning, as he was getting dressed and combing his hair in front of the mirror, she lay on the bed watching silently. Finally, she asked, "Sonny, how old are you?"

"I'm thirty-two," he said.

"Tell me something, then," she said. "Aren't you a little too old to believe in witches?"

It was his wedding night and the minister finished undressing in the bathroom and walked into the bedroom. He was surprised to see that his bride had already slipped between the bed sheets.

"My dear," he said, "I thought I would find you on your knees."

She said, "Well, honey, I can do it that way too, but it gives me the hiccoughs."

The newly-married Italian couple came home to Brooklyn from their honeymoon and moved into the upstairs apartment they'd rented from the groom's parents.

That night, the father of the groom was awakened from his deep sleep by his wife nudging him by hitting his stomach with her elbow. "Tony, listen!" she whispered.

He listened. Upstairs, the bed was creaking in rhythm.

The wife said, "Come on, Tony!" So Tony rolled on top of her and fucked her.

He was trying to fall back to sleep when, fifteen minutes later, the same sounds were heard. The wife said, "Tony! Listen to them! Come on, Tony!"

Once again, Tony got on top of her and fucked her.

A short time later, the bedsprings upstairs began to squeak again. And again the wife nudged her husband. "Tony, listen!" At this, Tony leaped from the bed, grabbed a broom, and banged the handle against the ceiling as he shouted, "Hey, kids, cut it out! You're killing your old man!"

So this husband from Roslyn Heights, Long Island, kissed his wife goodbye and got into his Cadillac to drive to work in New York City. He'd gone about a mile when he remembered that he'd left something in the bedroom. So he turned the car around and drove back home.

When he walked into the bedroom, there was his wife, lying totally nude on the bed and the milkman standing totally nude beside her.

The milkman promptly went into a squatting position on the rug and said, "I'm glad you're here, Mr. Jones, because I was just telling your wife that if she doesn't pay the milk bill, I'm gonna shit all over the floor."

A man who was very depressed met his friend Jerry J., who was a very sharp thinker.

"What's the matter?" Jerry J. asked.

"I'm despondent. I can't adjust to the fact that I've got three balls."

"Three balls?" said sharp Jerry. "Kid, we can make a fortune together!"

"How?" asked the other fellow, brightening up.

"We'll go to bar after bar and bet everybody around that between you and the bartender you've got five balls! It can't miss!"

"Let's go," said the man.

So they went into the first bar, and Jerry J. made friends with the strangers at the bar. Then he made the announcement: "I'll bet anybody in the place that between my friend here and the bartender they've got five balls."

Nearly everyone rushed forward to cover the bet.

Jerry looked at the bartender who was shaking his head.

"You don't mind being part of the wager; do you?" Jerry asked.

"Not at all," the bartender said. "I'm very impressed."

"How do you mean?" Jerry asked.

"Well, up to now I've never met a man with four balls. I've only got one."

A young farm boy from Arkansas was sent to New York by his father to learn the undertaking business under the tutelage of the great Frank E. Campbell.

Some months later, the father visited his son in the big city. "Tell me," he said, "have you learned much?"

"Oh sure, Dad," said the son. "I've learned a lot. And it's been very interesting."

"What was the most interesting thing you learned?"

The son thought for a minute and then said, "Well, we did have one wild experience that taught me a lesson."

"What was that?"

"Well," said the son, "one day we got this phone call from the Taft Hotel. It seems that the housekeeper had checked one of the rooms and she discovered that a man and woman had died in their sleep on the bed and completely naked."

"Wow!" said the father. "What did Mr. Campbell do?"

"Well, he put on his tuxedo and he had me put on my tuxedo. Then we were driven in one of his limousines to the Taft Hotel. The manager took us to the desk clerk who gave us the room number. Then the manager rode up with us in the elevator. We were silent because Mr. Campbell always believed in doing things with great dignity."

"How marvelous!" exclaimed the father. "Then what happened?"

"Well, we came to this room. Mr. Campbell pushed the door open with his gold-tipped cane. He, the manager, and I walked in quietly. Sure enough, there on the bed was this naked couple lying on their backs."

"And then what happened?" asked the father.

"Well, Mr. Campbell saw an immediate problem. The man had a large erection."

"And then what happened?" asked the father.

"Mr. Campbell, as usual, was up to the situation. He swung his gold-tipped cane and very stylishly whacked the penis."

"And then what happened?" asked the father.

"Well, Dad," said the son, "all hell broke loose. You see, we were in the wrong room!"

The Mother Superior in the convent school was chatting with her young charges and she asked them when they wanted to be when they grew up.

A twelve-year-old said, "I want to be a prostitute."

The Mother Superior fainted dead away on the spot. When they revived her, she raised her head from the ground and gasped, "What—did—you—say—?"

The young girl shrugged. "I said I want to be a prostitute."

"A prostitute!" the Mother Superior said. "Oh, praise sweet Jesus! And I thought you said you wanted to be a Protestant."

Little Jimmy had become a real nuisance while the men tried to concentrate on their Saturday afternoon poker game. His father tried in every way he could to get Jimmy to occupy himself, but the youngster insisted on running back and forth behind the players and calling out the cards they held.

The players became so annoyed that they threatened to quit the game. At this point, the boy's uncle stood up, took Jimmy by the hand, and led him out of the room. The uncle returned in a short time without Jimmy and without comment, and the game resumed.

For the balance of the afternoon, there was no trouble from Jimmy. After the game had ended and the players were settling their wins and losses, one of the men asked Jimmy's uncle, "What in the world did you do to Jimmy?"

"Not much," the boy's uncle replied. "I showed him how to jerk off."

The bridegroom carried his bride over the threshold and into the honeymoon suite. They had taken off all their clothes, when suddenly the sweet young thing began to tremble.

"What's the matter, honey?" he asked in a concerned voice.

She was now shivering all over. "I've got an attack of St. Vitus Dance," she said.

The groom thought about it for a minute, then picked up the hotel phone and called the bell captain for help.

Four bellboys came rushing into the room.

"Quick! You grab her arms," the young man shouted to two of them. To the other two, he directed, "Grab her legs and hold her tight."

He leaped into the bed on top of her, inserted his penis into her, and then shouted to the straining bellboys, "Okay, fellows, let her go!"

A Frenchman who was leaving his home in Paris for a few weeks confided in his friend, Pierre: "I always hate to leave the city. When I'm away, I just don't know what my wife is doing. There's always the doubt, always the doubt."

Pierre said, "Charles, I'll tell you what. Because we're such good friends, I'll keep an eye on her every evening that you're gone."

"Would you do that for me?" Charles said, obviously delighted and relieved. He kissed Pierre on both cheeks. "You understand, dear friend, that I know I should trust my wife. It's just that there's always the doubt, always the doubt."

"Have no fear, Pierre will be there," the friend said.

Three weeks later, Charles returned to Paris and the two men met.

"Charles, I'm afraid I have bad news for you," Pierre said.

"Well?"

"The very first night you were gone, I watched this man go to your house. Your wife opened the door and kissed and hugged him. He fondled her breast. He rubbed her crotch. Then they closed the door to go upstairs. Never daunted, I climbed the tree outside your house and I observed them closely from one of its branches."

"And so—?" said Charles.

"Well, first they took off all their clothes. Incidentally, dear friend, your wife has a lovely body."

"She does, indeed," said Charles thoughtfully. "What happened then?"

"Then?" Pierre shook his head sorrowfully. "Then is when they turned out the light. I could see nothing. I could learn nothing more."

Charles sighed a deep sigh. "So you see how it is, my friend? Always the doubt, always the doubt."

Two factory workers were at their lathes and one of them said, "Listen, are you going to the hockey game tomorrow night? You know, it's the big game. The Rangers are playing Montreal."

"Naw," said the other one, "my wife won't let me go."

"You're a fool. There's nothing to it."

"What do you mean?"

"Well, an hour before the game you simply pick her up, carry her to the bed, fling her on the bed, tear off her clothes, fuck her, and say, 'I'm going to the hockey game'!"

The following Monday, the two men met at work and the first one said, "What happened? I didn't see you at the game. Didn't you do what I suggested?"

The second man said: "I'll tell you how it was. An hour before the game, I picked up the wife, carried her to the bedroom, and flung her onto the bed."

"Yes?"

"And then, just as I was pulling off her panties and opening my fly, I thought to myself, what the hell, Montreal hasn't been playing that well lately."

The judge came home and found his wife in bed with his very best friend.

"Hey, what do you think you're doing?"

"See," the wife said to the man beside her, "I told you he was stupid."

This seedy looking girl walked into a seedy looking bar. A couple of seedy looking customers stood at the other end.

"Gimme a Rheingold," she said.

She took the glass of beer and swallowed it with one gulp. Then she fell to the floor in a dead faint.

"Come, give me a hand," the bartender called. The two men helped the bartender carry her into the back room. One of the men glanced around and said, "Listen. Nobody'll know. How about we all give her a quick fuck?"

They did just that. An hour or so later, she came to and said, "Where am I? What time is it? I've got to get home." And out she went.

Next afternoon, there were six men hanging around the bar when the same girl came in, walked up to the bartender and said, "Gimme a Rheingold."

She drank it down in one gulp and then fell to the floor in a dead faint.

The men carried her to the back room and the fucking performance was repeated, except that now there were seven, including the bartender.

The next day when she came in, there were twenty-four men, all waiting around.

"Gimme a Rheingold," she said. She swallowed it

in one gulp, fell to the floor in a dead faint, and was carried to the back room, where all twenty-four men partook of her.

When she arrived on the fourth day, the word had really gotten around, and there were more than seventy men in the bar, waiting eagerly with lustful eyes and eager cocks. As she walked up to the bar, the bartender pushed a glass of beer toward her.

"You want your Rheingold, Miss?" he said.

"No," she said. "You better give me a Schlitz. That Rheingold gives me a pain in the cunt."

He was very wealthy and very old—in fact, he was about to celebrate his eighty-third birthday. He went to the doctor for a checkup. The doctor gave him a thorough going-over, and then said, "For a man who's about to be eighty-three, you're in marvelous shape. But why a physical just a day before your birthday?"

The wealthy old man explained that that very afternoon he was going to marry an eighteen-year-old girl.

The doctor tried with a great deal of effort to dissuade him. "I'm goin' ahead with it no matter what," the old man said. "Got any other suggestions, Doc?"

"Just one. If you want a really peaceful marriage, I suggest that you take in a boarder."

The old man thought about it and said that it sounded like a good idea.

The next time the doctor met the old man it was at a fund-raising affair, half a year later. The old man came up to him and said, "Doctor, congratulate me! My wife's pregnant!"

The doctor tried to maintain his poise, and said, "Well, so at least you followed my good advice and took in a boarder."

"Oh, sure," said the old man, with a wicked grin, "and the boarder's pregnant as well!"

Once upon a time there was a sperm named Stanley who lived inside a famous movie actor. Stanley was a very healthy sperm. He'd do pushups and somersaults and limber himself up all the time, while the other sperm just lay around on their fat asses not doing a thing.

One day, one of them because curious enough to ask Stanley why he exercised all day.

Stanley said, "Look, pal, only one sperm gets a woman pregnant and when the right time comes, I am going to be that one."

A few days later, they all felt themselves getting hotter and hotter, and they knew that it was getting to be their time to go. They were released abruptly and, sure enough, there was Stanley swimming far ahead of all the others.

All of a sudden, Stanley stopped, turned around, and began to swim back with all his might. "Go back! Go back!" he screamed. "It's a blow job!"

He was on his way home when he came upon a woman crying hysterically. "What's the matter, lady?" he asked.

She could only sob, "Schultz is dead. Schultz is dead!"

He shook his head and continued walking. Suddenly he came upon another woman sobbing, "Schultz is dead, Schultz is dead!"

He couldn't get over it because soon he came upon another woman crying the same thing. He had never seen so many unhappy women. And then he came upon a scene that caused him to stop. A trolley car had run over a man and had cut him to pieces. There, on the pavement next to the body, was this foot-and-a-half-long penis, and a half-dozen women were standing around crying hysterically, "Schultz is dead. Schultz is dead!"

When he arrived home, he greeted his wife with, "I just saw the damndest thing. A trolley car ran over a man and cut off his cock, and would you believe it, the cock was a foot and a half long."

"Oh my God!" the wife screamed, "Schultz is dead. Schultz is dead!"

Marilyn had a parrot for a pet, but the parrot would embarrass her whenever she came into the apartment with a man. He would shout all kinds of obscenities, always leading off with "Somebody's gonna get it tonight! Somebody's gonna get it tonight!"

In desperation, Marilyn went to her local pet shop and explained her parrot problem to the pet shop proprietor.

"What you need," he said, "is a female parrot too. I don't have one on hand, but I'll order one. Meanwhile, you could borrow this female owl until the female parrot arrives."

Marilyn took the owl home and put it near her parrot. It was immediately obvious that the parrot didn't care for the owl. He glared at it.

The night, Marilyn wasn't her usual nervous self as she opened the door to bring her gentleman friend in for a nightcap. Then suddenly she heard the parrot screech and she knew that things hadn't changed.

"Somebody's gonna get it tonight! Somebody's gonna get it tonight!" the parrot said.

The owl said, "Whoo? Whoo?"

And the parrot said, "Not you, you big-eyed son-of-a-bitch!"

No one who buys it,
survives it.

THE HOUSE NEXT DOOR

A terrifying novel
by
Anne Rivers Siddons

28172 $2.25

Coming in November

 BALLANTINE BOOKS

G-1

Bestsellers from BALLANTINE